Oakland A's slugger Jose Canseco steals two bases against Milwaukee. The 24-year-old becomes the first ballplayer in history to hit 40 homers and steal 40 bases in one season.

Mike Schmidt steps up to the plate in Pittsburgh. The Phillies are trailing the Pirates with one man on and two outs in the ninth inning. With one swing of the bat, Mike wins the game for Philadelphia with a home run. He becomes only the 14th player in baseball history to hit 500 homers.

Don Mattingly slugs home runs in eight straight ball games. He ties a 31-year-old big league record set by Dale Long of the Pirates. During the streak, Don hits .459 with 21 RBIs.

These and other stories are in this book about today's superstar hitters of major league baseball—from George Brett and Wade Boggs to Kirby Puckett and Darryl Strawberry. Great Hall-of-Famers like Hank Aaron and Joe DiMaggio are also spotlighted.

It all adds up to exciting and entertaining reading for young baseball fans everywhere.

Great Sports Heroes books from Tor

SPORTS HEROES:
GREAT HITTERS

P.R. EMERT

TOR

A TOM DOHERTY ASSOCIATES BOOK
NEW YORK

FOR LISA, RICK, AND HOLLY

SPORTS HEROES: GREAT HITTERS

Copyright © 1990 by RGA Publishing Group, Inc.

A Tor Book
Published by Tom Doherty Associates, Inc.
49 West 24th Street
New York, N.Y. 10010

ISBN: 0-812-59379-0   Can. ISBN: 0-812-59380-4

First edition: February 1990

Printed in the United States of America

0 9 8 7 6 5 4 3 2 1

★ TABLE OF CONTENTS ★

★ WADE BOGGS ★

SEPTEMBER 20, 1988 WAS A HISTORIC DAY IN MAJOR league baseball. The Boston Red Sox led the second-place Milwaukee Brewers by five games in the Eastern Division of the American League.

The Red Sox were playing the Toronto Blue Jays. A Boston win would lower their magic number to seven with eleven games to go in the season. (Red Sox wins and Brewer losses totaling seven would clinch the title for Boston.)

It wasn't the pennant race that attracted the Toronto fans. They came to the ballpark to see baseball history made. The greatest batter in the game had 198 hits. The fans wanted to see third baseman Wade Boggs of the Red Sox collect number 200.

Boston went on top early with four runs in the first inning. As the leadoff hitter, Wade started the rally by lining a single for his 199th hit.

It was 4–1 when he came to bat again in the fourth inning. Wade faced Blue Jays lefthander Jeff Musselman. Wasting little time, the man called "the toughest out in baseball" grounded another single to left field. He had reached the magic 200!

Wade Boggs became the first player in this century to get 200 hits in six straight seasons. (Wee Willie Keeler did it for eight straight years from 1894 to 1901.)

The Red Sox won the game 13–2. A few days later they clinched the Eastern Division title but lost in the American League playoffs to Oakland.

Wade had a spectacular record-breaking season in 1988. He hit .366 to win the league batting title for the fourth straight year. His lifetime batting average of .356 over seven seasons tied him for third place with Shoeless Joe Jackson. Only Ty Cobb (.367) and Rogers Hornsby (.358) have better career averages.

Wade also joined Lou Gehrig as the only players to collect 200 hits and 100 walks in three straight seasons. In 1988 Wade had 214 hits, five home runs and 58 RBIs (runs batted in). He led the American League with 125 walks, 128 runs, 45 doubles and a .476 on-base percentage. Nearly half of the time he came to the plate he ended up on base!

Wade Anthony Boggs was born June 15, 1958, in Omaha, Nebraska. His father was an Air Force master sergeant and his mother was a pilot.

His family life was very disciplined. "Dinner was at 5:30," explained Wade, "and if you weren't home, you didn't eat."

Mr. Boggs started to play baseball with Wade

when he was still in diapers. "He was about 18 months old," recalled his dad. "I pitched to him in the backyard with a plastic ball and bat ... even then he had good hand-eye coordination."

His dad became his coach and encouraged Wade to bat lefthanded and throw righthanded. At the age of six he decided to become a baseball player. By the time he was ten, Mr. Boggs thought Wade could make it to the big leagues.

His mother said, "He was born to hit like some kids are born to play the piano."

In Little League and American Legion ball, Wade played shortstop. By the time he was finished at H. B. Plant High School in Tampa, Florida, he had won All-Conference, All-State, and All-American honors. As a junior, Wade was the best hitter in the state, batting .522 with eight homers and 41 RBIs.

The talented young athlete was also an All-State punter in football and an honor student. After graduating from high school, he was selected by the Boston Red Sox in the seventh round of the 1976 draft.

For six years (from age 18 to 24) Wade played minor league baseball, switching from shortstop to third base. He went from the A club to AA ball and finally to the Boston AAA team at Pawtucket, Rhode Island.

He was an excellent hitter, batting over .300 for five straight years in the minors. But the coaches felt Wade needed more work on his fielding and running. They wanted him to hit with more power.

He was finally brought up to the Red Sox in 1982. When third baseman Carney Lansford was injured, Wade moved into the starting lineup and has been there ever since.

In seven years in the major leagues, Wade has never batted below .325. He won the league batting title in 1983 (.361), 1985 (.368), 1986 (.357), 1987 (.363) and 1988 (.366).

The Red Sox won their division in 1986 and beat the Angels for the American League pennant. They lost to the New York Mets in the seventh game of the World Series.

Wade has been described as "the best two-strike hitter in history." He often takes two strikes because he wants to see what the pitcher has to offer before he swings.

The 6'2" 197-pound athlete learned early that the key to good hitting was practice and discipline. During the entire 1988 season Wade went three straight games without a hit only twice. The other players have called him a "hitting machine."

"My goal is to hit the ball as hard and as consistently as I can," he said. "Too many players lose it all when they reach for the home run."

Many wonder whether the talented third baseman can reach the magic .400 mark in batting. The last player to accomplish this was Ted Williams in 1941.

Could the 31-year-old eventually have the highest lifetime batting average in major league history? His present .356 career average is only 11 points shy of the great Ty Cobb. The next few years will provide answers to these questions.

A certain Hall-of-Famer, Wade and his wife, Debbie, have two children.

KISS IT GOODBYE: Boston Red Sox's Wade Boggs jumps on a Mets pitch during the second game of the 1986 World Series.

★ GEORGE BRETT ★

THE PRESSURE WAS ON THE KANSAS CITY ROYALS the night of October 11, 1985. It was the League Championship Series and the Toronto Blue Jays had already won the first two games. The Royals had lost ten straight postseason games dating back to the 1980 World Series.

Kansas City needed an outstanding performance from one of their veteran players. It was their third baseman, George Brett, who came through for them.

In the first inning, the 32-year-old hit a bases-empty homer. In the fourth, he doubled and scored a run. After the Blue Jays exploded for five runs in the fifth, George promptly belted a two-run homer in the sixth to tie the score at 5–5.

The veteran stroked a single in the eighth between first base and second. After a sacrifice groundout and walk, he scored the winning run on a bloop hit by Steve Balboni. It was George who caught the final out of the game, a popup in foul territory. In four at-bats, the popular slugger had four hits (a double, single, and two home runs), three RBIs, and scored four runs.

"That's a Hall of Fame performance," declared Royals manager Dick Howser.

That year Kansas City beat Toronto in the League Championship. George batted .370 in the World Series and the Royals were victorious over the St. Louis Cardinals in seven games.

1985 was a tremendous year for the 6' 200-pound athlete. He won his first Gold Glove award, batted .335 (second in the league), collected 184 hits, 30 home runs, and 112 RBIs.

George Howard Brett was born May 15, 1953, in Glendale, West Virginia. The Bretts moved to Hermosa Beach, California in 1955.

George and his three brothers grew up playing all sports. At El Segundo High School, he starred in baseball and football. But it was baseball that the Brett boys loved best. One brother, Ken, went on to pitch in the major leagues. The others, John and Bobby, both played minor league ball.

George was drafted by the Kansas City Royals in 1971 and assigned to their minor league club in Billings, Montana. The 18-year-old hit .291 and played shortstop. In 1972 he batted .274 for San Jose in the California League.

At the Royals' AAA club in Omaha, Nebraska, George switched to third base and batted .284. He was called up to Kansas City during the last 13 games of the 1973 season. Only 20 years old at the time, George was the youngest Royal ever

7

to make a big league appearance. He went one for four in that game, lining a single to left field. It was the first major league hit of his career.

George opened the 1974 season at Omaha but, after sixteen games, joined the Royals for good on May 3. That year he batted .282 and collected 129 hits. But he had only two home runs and 47 RBIs.

Royals batting instructor Charlie Lau taught George how to hit with power to all fields. Lau focused on ten points for good hitting. They included common advice such as "Don't try to hit a home run. Keep your eye on the ball. Keep your head still. Wait on the ball. Make a level swing. Use the whole field. Relax." George followed Lau's advice in practice day after day.

In 1975 he batted .308, led the league in hits (195) and tied for the league lead in triples (13). George batted in 89 runs and belted 11 home runs. In 1976 the talented third baseman led the league in batting (.333), hits (215), triples (14), total bases (298), and at-bats (645).

Over the years George has continued to be one of the American League's top players. But one year stands out among the best batting performances in baseball history.

In 1980 George batted an incredible .390, the highest in the big leagues since Ted Williams hit .406 in 1941. The veteran slugger became the first player in thirty years to average one RBI in each game, batting in 118 runs in 117 games.

George belted 24 home runs and struck out only 22 times during the entire season. He led the Royals into the League Championship Series. His two home runs helped Kansas City defeat the Yankees for their first American League pennant. Despite George's .375 batting average and four extra-base hits in the World Series, the Royals lost to Philadelphia. Among other honors, he was named the League Most Valuable Player (MVP).

In his 15-year major league career, George has compiled a .310 batting average. He has been selected to play in 13 All-Star Games, more than any other active player in baseball. He's led the league twice in batting, three times in hits, twice in total bases, once in doubles, and three times in triples. He's had 10 seasons in which he batted over .300, and he has won a Gold Glove.

Yet George has been bothered with injuries throughout his career. He's missed games because of back pain, a broken toe, tendinitis of the wrist, bone chips in the thumb, a bruised heel, torn hamstring, torn knee ligaments and a sore shoulder. Many of his injuries were the result of playing on the hard turf at Royals Stadium, which was finally replaced in 1985.

Some might have expected the 36-year-old to slow down over the years. Now at first base, George finished the 1988 season proving he is still one of the best players in the game. He played in 157 games, batted .306 with 24 homers and 103 RBIs. He had 42 doubles and stole 14 bases. George didn't go more than two games without a hit all year!

Certain to be selected to the Hall of Fame after he retires, George credits his knowledge of baseball to former Kansas City manager Whitey Herzog (now manager of the St. Louis Cardinals).

"Whitey taught me not to get too excited when things were good," he explained, "and not to be too depressed when they were bad."

George is single and lives in Southern California. He and his brothers own two minor league ball clubs in the Northwest League.

HIT THE GROUND RUNNING: Kansas City Royals slugger George Brett belts one for a double in his first at-bat in the first inning of the opening game of the 1980 American League playoffs against the New York Yankees.

★ JOSE CANSECO ★

ELECTRICITY WAS IN THE AIR AT MILWAUKEE COUNTY Stadium on September 23, 1988. It wasn't an ordinary baseball game between the Brewers and the Oakland Athletics. The home team needed a win to stay in the race for the Eastern Division title.

But the crowd was buzzing about something else. They hoped to be eyewitnesses to a historic event in baseball. 24-year-old Jose Canseco of the A's would attempt to become the first ballplayer in history to hit 40 homers and steal 40 bases in one season.

Power and speed is an unusual combination in baseball. Only 10 players have ever hit 30 home runs and stolen 30 bases in one season. Two major leaguers came close to breaking the 40/40 barrier. In 1973 Bobby Bonds of San Francisco had 39 homers and 43 stolen bases. In 1987

Eric Davis of Cincinnati hit 37 homers and stole 50 bases in only 129 games.

Jose set the 40/40 goal for himself when the season began in April. By August 6 he had hit 31 roundtrippers and stolen 30 bases. The young slugger belted his 40th home run on September 18. Now he needed only two stolen bases to stand alone in the record books!

Jose came to bat against Brewers pitcher Juan Nieves in the first inning. Without a delay, he stroked a single. The crowd cheered him on to steal second.

Into the batter's box came Mark McGwire. Jose took his lead, and on the second pitch to the plate he took off at high speed. The throw to second wasn't even close. The talented athlete had stolen #39!

In the fifth inning Jose batted again. He took the Brewers and fans by surprise when he bunted a dribbler towards third. The speedy slugger reached first base safely. It was the first time he had bunted for a hit in the 1988 season.

The crowd chanted, "Go, go, go." On the pitch to Mark McGwire, Jose did just that. He raced to second, beating the catcher's throw easily. He had stolen his 40th base of the season and made baseball history!

The crowd went wild. The applause was thunderous. The game was stopped and Jose was presented with second base to put in his trophy case. The young and gifted athlete went on to hit his 41st home run that night. The Athletics beat the Brewers 9–8 in 14 innings.

Jose finished the 1988 season with some incredible statistics. He batted .307 (9th best in the American League). He belted 42 home runs (first in the majors) and batted in 124 runs (also first in the majors).

Jose scored 120 runs (2nd in the majors), was fourth in the league in stolen bases (40), and smacked 187 hits (6th in the league). It was only natural that he was unanimously selected as the American League MVP.

The A's finished first in the Western Division. They had the best record in baseball, 104 wins and 58 losses. After beating Boston for the League Championship, they lost in the World Series to the Los Angeles Dodgers.

Jose Canseco was born on July 2, 1964, in Havana, Cuba. When he and his twin brother, Osvaldo, were nine months old, Mr. Canseco moved the family to Miami, Florida.

The identical twins were skinny, tall kids who grew up playing baseball in southwest Miami. Both attended Coral Park High School.

"I was 6'1" and 155 pounds when I started high school," explained Jose. "I didn't play on the varsity baseball team until my senior year."

That year he hit .400 and an A's scout in Miami noticed the young outfielder. Oakland selected him in the 15th round of the 1982 draft.

The 18-year-old played for seven different minor league teams from 1982 to 1985. He didn't become a real power hitter until 1984 when he began to lift weights. Jose added 35 pounds of muscle to his 6'3" frame and weighed in at 230 pounds. He's one of the strongest players in the game today and can bench press 400 pounds.

With his added strength came home runs and a better batting average. The 21-year-old exploded in 1985 while playing for AA Huntsville, Alabama and AAA Tacoma, Washington. Jose

14

batted well over .300 with 36 home runs. The roundtrippers were tape measure shots and his reputation grew.

The young outfielder was promoted to the A's in late 1985. In 29 games that year he batted .302 with five home runs and 13 RBIs. In his official rookie season in 1986, Jose's batting average slipped but his power hitting continued. He batted .240 with 33 homers and 117 RBIs. The talented right fielder was named Rookie of the Year.

Jose worked hard to improve his average and cut down on his strikeouts. In 1987 he accomplished both, batting .257 with 31 home runs and 113 RBIs.

After his outstanding 1988 season Jose declared that he wants "to improve (his) batting average, home run total, stolen bases and," he added, "cut strikeouts down to 100."

"I'm really just an easygoing guy with a good sense of humor," he explained. "I just let things fall where they may."

Jose is married. He and his wife, Esther, live in Miami.

ROUTINE MIRACLES: Jose Canseco of the Oakland A's hits his major-league-leading 26th home run of the 1988 season, en route to Oakland's 4–1 victory over the Detroit Tigers.

★ WILL CLARK ★

THE SAN FRANCISCO GIANTS TRAILED THE SAN DI-
ego Padres 7–4 in the bottom of the ninth inning. It was June 22, 1988. Some fans in
Candlestick Park were already heading for the
exits.

The Giants rallied for one run but now there
were two outs with the bases loaded. With the
winning run on first base, infielder Will Clark
stepped up to the plate. He faced former Giants
pitcher Mark Davis.

Will battled Davis pitch after pitch until finally the count was full—three balls and two
strikes. The runners were going on the next
pitch.

Davis wound up and threw a fastball on the
outside corner of the plate. Will swung the bat
and made contact. He lined Davis's pitch deep
down the right field line in fair territory.

17

The Giants' fans started screaming. San Diego right fielder Tony Gwynn rushed over to get the ball and fired it in to the cutoff man. San Francisco runners were circling the bases as fast as they could. One run scored! Two runs scored!

Chris Speier rounded third and raced to the plate with the winning run. The Padre cutoff man fired the ball home. Speier slid in just ahead of the tag! The run scored and the Giants won the game 8–7.

This come-from-behind victory was the greatest single day of Will Clark's career in baseball. Against the Padres, he went four for five with one single, two doubles, and one home run. Will also scored one run and collected seven RBIs.

The young ballplayer sizzled in June and was named the National League Player of the month. The Giants finished the season in fourth place in the Western Division. They had an 83–79 record.

Will had an outstanding year in 1988. He batted .282, belted 29 home runs and had 109 RBIs.

William Nuschler Clark, Jr. was born on March 13, 1964, in New Orleans, Louisiana. "I'm a third-generation native of New Orleans," he explained, "and I went to the same high school as my dad."

Will played basketball and baseball at Jesuit High. In his senior year he was an All-American and played in Babe Ruth and American Legion ball.

After graduation in 1982, Will attended Mississippi State University. The 6'1" athlete was named a National Collegiate Athletic Association (NCAA) All-American at MSU. In 61 ballgames he batted .386 with 28 home runs and 92 RBIs.

In 1984 Will was selected to the United States Olympic Team. Before the Games, the squad went on a 35-game tour throughout the country. Will batted .393 with 13 homers and 35 RBIs while on tour.

During the Olympics, the young Americans won the silver medal. Will was a standout, batting .429 in five games with three home runs and eight RBIs.

In 1985 the talented young athlete was named the winner of the Golden Spikes Award as the best collegiate baseball player in the country. Will led MSU into the College World Series after hitting .420 with 25 home runs and 77 RBIs that season.

The San Francisco Giants made Will their number one pick in the June, 1985 free agent draft. He was assigned to the Fresno, California A farm club. In his first at-bat as a professional on June 21 he hit a home run!

After only 65 games in class A ball, Will was brought directly up to the big leagues. In 1986, the 22-year-old became the starting first baseman for San Francisco. In his first major league at-bat, Will hit a home run off Nolan Ryan of the Houston Astros.

During his rookie year Will hit .287 for the Giants with eleven home runs and 41 RBIs. An injured left elbow forced him to miss 47 games during the season. He had successful surgery on the elbow in October, 1986.

The young slugger had an outstanding year in 1987. Will (nicknamed "The Thrill") hit .308 with 35 homers and 91 RBIs. His teammates voted him the Giants' MVP after they became Western Division champions.

The Giants lost to the St. Louis Cardinals in the seventh game of the National League Championship Series. Will hit .360 in the losing effort.

He became the seventh player in Giants history to hit 30 or more home runs and bat .300 or better in the same season. (The others are Mel Ott, Johnny Mize, Walker Cooper, Willie Mays, Orlando Cepeda, and Willie McCovey.)

The 25-year-old had another super year in 1988. Will was intentionally walked 27 times—more than any other player in baseball. His 109 RBIs were the most by a Giant since Willie McCovey drove in 127 runs in 1970.

The Thrill became the third player in Giants history to complete the "triple-triple" (100+ runs, 100+ RBIs, and 100+ walks). Only Mel Ott and Willie McCovey have ever done it before.

Some believe Will has the best natural swing in baseball. He's been compared to Stan Musial and Don Mattingly.

Will models himself on George Brett of the Kansas City Royals. "He hits the ball to all fields with power for a high average," Will once said. "I've been successful at doing that, too."

The young first baseman has excellent 20–13 vision in both eyes (20–20 is normal). He's talkative, confident, and emotional. "I'm a line-drive hitter with power," declared Will, "and there's not a shy bone in this body!"

FLAT OUT: First baseman Will Clark of the San Francisco Giants dives for a ball hit by Cincinnati Reds shortstop Kurt Stillwell.

★ ANDRE DAWSON ★

THE PHILADELPHIA PHILLIES CAME INTO CHICAGO ON August 1, 1987, with a five-game winning streak on the line. They looked forward to belting the ball around the natural grass at Wrigley Field.

Cubs outfielder Andre Dawson was having a great year but he lined into a double play in the first inning. The Phillies were confident they could shut down "Awesome Dawson." They were wrong!

Andre came to the plate in the third inning with two men on base. He hammered a Tom Hume pitch into the left field bleachers.

Leading off the fifth inning, Andre belted another Hume pitch into the left field seats. The Cubs took the lead 4–3. He came to bat again in the 7th inning. This time Andre faced Phillies pitcher Mike Jackson. The fans in left field watched carefully. They weren't disappointed.

The 6'3" 195-pound athlete swung at a waist-high fastball. It took off and cleared the left field wall. It was Andre's third straight home run of the game!

The Cubs beat the Phillies 5–3. Andre had three of the team's seven hits. He scored three runs and drove in all five runs in the game.

It was an awesome show in a year which was the greatest of his 11-year major league career. He batted .287, slugged 49 home runs, and had 137 runs batted in. Andre led the majors in RBIs and tied Oakland's Mark McGwire for the home run lead.

The Cubs finished in sixth place in 1987, but Andre was selected the Most Valuable Player in the National League. It was the first MVP award ever given to a member of a last-place team!

In 1987 Andre earned his seventh Gold Glove for fielding. He was selected the National League Player of the Year and was a starter in the All-Star Game.

Andre Nolan Dawson was born on July 10, 1954, in South Miami, Florida. The oldest of eight children, he practiced baseball in the streets by hitting rocks that his brother threw. Instead of a bat, he used broom and mop handles. Andre explained to his mother that he was practicing to become a baseball player.

He was active in sports at Southwest Miami Senior High School. Andre graduated in 1972 and attended college at Florida A & M University. After three years, he was selected by the Montreal Expos in the 1975 free agent draft.

Andre played 72 games for Lethbridge, Canada of the Pioneer (Rookie A) League. He batted .330 with 13 home runs and 50 RBIs. He started the 1976 minor league season at Quebec, Canada of the Eastern (AA) League. In only 40 games, the tall, slim outfielder batted .357 with eight homers and 27 RBIs.

Finally, Andre was promoted to Denver, Colorado, the Expos' AAA club of the American Association. He continued to play excellent baseball. In 74 games he batted .350 with 20 home runs and 46 RBIs.

By the 1977 season, the talented young athlete was in the big leagues as the starting center fielder for Montreal. He won the National League Rookie of the Year award by batting .282 with 65 RBIs and 19 home runs.

In his ten years with the Expos (from 1977 through 1986) he was Montreal's all-time leader in home runs, hits, doubles, triples, runs scored, total bases and at-bats.

Nicknamed "Hawk," Andre has had knee problems throughout his career since he hurt himself playing high school football. At the end of the 1986 season the Expos decided to cut his salary. They said it was because of his weakened knees and his advancing age (33). Andre was insulted and became a free agent. Surprisingly, no other team wanted him.

Hawk liked the idea of playing for Chicago. The natural grass at Wrigley Field was easier on his injured knees. He also enjoyed playing daytime baseball. The Cubs played most of their home games during the day. (Andre's batting average in the daytime was nearly 50 points higher than under the lights at night).

He took a chance and showed up at the Cubs training camp in Arizona. Hawk refused to take "no" for an answer. He agreed to play for Chicago for only one-quarter of what he was getting at Montreal. The Cubs got their money's worth and more.

Andre's incredible 1987 season made him a superstar in the Windy City. The Cubs increased his salary equal to his amazing performance. "My biggest satisfaction," he said, "was showing the people in Montreal that they made a mistake!"

1988 was an improved year for Chicago. They led the National League in hitting as a team. The Cubs finished fourth in the Eastern Division with a 77–85 record.

Andre had another outstanding season. With a .303 average, he was third in the league in batting. He ranked first in multi-hit games (57) and second in hits (179) and total bases (298).

Andre batted in 79 runs and slugged 24 homers during the 1988 season. Against his former team, Montreal, he went 27 for 54, batting .500. For the second straight year, the talented outfielder homered in his final Wrigley Field at-bat.

In a game between the Expos and the Cubs on September 24, 1985, Andre made major league history. He belted three homers for Montreal and had eight RBIs as the Expos beat Chicago 17–15.

What made Andre's performance a standout was that he hit two home runs in one inning! And it was the second time he had done it! The first was on July 30, 1978. No other major leaguer has ever smashed two roundtrippers in the same inning twice!

Andre and his wife, Vanessa, live in Chicago and Miami.

ONE GOOD TRY: Montreal Expo Andre Dawson gets tagged in spite of his leap over St. Louis Cardinals' catcher Tom Nieto.

★ TONY GWYNN ★

IT WAS EARLY IN THE 1987 BASEBALL SEASON WHEN Tony Gwynn had the kind of day most players only dream about. The San Diego Padres were playing the Los Angeles Dodgers on April 16.

The game was tied 2–2 when Tony stepped up to the plate in the 10th inning. He had already had a tremendous day. Tony was four for four with two doubles and two singles.

The San Diego outfielder took his position in the batter's box, facing Dodger pitcher Matt Young. Wasting little time, Tony lined a single over the shortstop and got his fifth hit of the day.

Carmelo Martinez then smashed a fair ball down the left field line into the Padres bullpen. Tony raced around second and then rounded third. The ballgame was on the line and he knew it.

He slid into home plate, beating the relay from the outfield. Tony scored the winning run as the Padres beat the Dodgers 3–2!

This game was just a preview of the excellent season Tony was to have in 1987. He had the greatest single offensive year in the history of the San Diego Padres.

Tony's career high .370 batting average and 218 hits for the season led the major leagues. If he had gotten 18 more hits with the same number of at-bats, Tony would have been the first .400 hitter since Ted Williams in 1941.

He set five new Padre records, in batting average, hits, runs scored (119), triples (13), and intentional walks (26).

Tony reached base safely in 92% of the 157 games he played in. He didn't go more than two straight games without collecting at least one hit! His 56 stolen bases for the season was second in the National League and a career high.

In addition to his outstanding hitting Tony won a Gold Glove for his fielding. He was also selected to play in the All-Star Game. The 5'11" 200-pound athlete was the only bright spot in a poor San Diego season. The Padres finished last in the National League Western Division with a 65–97 record.

Anthony Keith Gwynn was born May 9, 1960 in Los Angeles, California. He grew up in Long Beach with his two brothers.

"We'd cut up socks, put rubber bands around them and call them baseballs," Tony explained. "I figured if you could hit one of those things, you could hit a real baseball."

Tony played high school basketball and baseball. After graduation he went to San Diego

State University on a basketball scholarship. As a point guard for the Aztec team Tony still holds the all-time assists record. He was good enough in basketball to be drafted by the San Diego (now Los Angeles) Clippers.

Tony didn't play baseball in college until his second year. At that time he used a large, 34-ounce bat. He believed that the bigger the bat, the longer the hit.

He tried a lighter, smaller bat and in his last two college seasons, Tony batted .423 and .416. To this day, he still uses a 31-ounce bat which some players describe as "a toothpick."

Tony was selected in the third round of the June, 1981 draft by the San Diego Padres. He played in the minor leagues for the Padres A team (Walla Walla, Washington) and then for Amarillo, Texas (AA).

In 1982 Tony played with Hawaii, San Diego's AAA club. On July 19 he was brought up to the major leagues. In his first game against Philadelphia, the young rookie got two hits!

On August 25 Tony broke his left wrist after diving for a ball, and missed three weeks. Then while playing winter ball in 1983 he broke his right wrist. This time he missed six months.

After a short time back with the AAA club now in Las Vegas, Nevada, Tony rejoined the Padres in June of '83. He hit .309 in 86 games with 94 hits, 37 RBIs and one home run.

It wasn't until 1984 that Tony played his first full season with San Diego. It was a memorable year. Tony led the major leagues with a .351 average, 213 hits, and 69 multiple-hit games. He

29

became the first Padre to ever get more than 200 hits in one season!

San Diego won their division in 1984. In the League Championship Series against the Cubs, Tony batted .368. His two-run double in the seventh inning of the fifth game won the National League pennant for the Padres. It was the first championship in the history of the club. (They eventually lost to Detroit in the World Series).

Tony's .317 batting average in 1985 was fourth in the National League. Some say he had an "off year," gathering only 197 hits. An off-year for Tony was an outstanding year for any other player.

1986 marked the season he won the first Gold Glove of his career. On August 27, he threw out three Mets from the outfield. Tony gunned down one man at the plate and two at second base to tie a club record for one game.

The talented outfielder batted .329 that year with 211 hits, 107 runs and 37 steals. In a September 21 game against the Houston Astros, Tony stole five bases. He became only the fifth man since 1900 to do so.

After his tremendous 1987 season Tony came right back in 1988 to win his second straight batting title with a .313 average. He did this despite playing with an injured left hand.

In 1988, Tony became the Padres' all-time hit leader. After 6½ seasons at San Diego, the 29-year-old has a .325 career batting average. In his last five years, he's averaged 200 hits per season.

Tony works hard to improve his game. "I want to be a complete player," he said. "I want to be consistent offensively and defensively. I feel good because I've been blessed with the ability to hit a baseball."

Tony is married. He and his wife, Alicia, have two children.

DOIN' WHAT YOU CAN: San Diego Padres out-fielder Tony Gwynn led the National League in batting during the 1987 season, even though the Padres spent the first half of the season in the basement.

★ DON MATTINGLY ★

GAME AFTER GAME, THE HOME RUNS SOARED OUT OF the ball park. Yankee slugger Don Mattingly belted fastballs, curveballs, and knuckleballs into the bleachers.

It started on July 8, 1987. The powerful first baseman had only eight home runs for the whole season. Then he blasted a pair of roundtrippers against the Minnesota Twins at Yankee Stadium. In the next four home games against the Chicago White Sox, Don slugged a home run in each game.

The sports world began to take notice. The talented Yankee had hit home runs in five straight games! After a break for the All-Star Game, Don faced the Texas Rangers. He belted two home runs and tied the American League record of homering in six straight games.

The next night Don faced Ranger lefthander

Paul Kilgus. He blasted another rocket out of the park as the Yankees won 8–4.

Don couldn't explain his seven-game homer streak. "They just seem to be happening," he said, "and I don't know why."

The record was set in May, 1956 by Dale Long of the Pittsburgh Pirates. He hit a home run in eight straight games. No major leaguer had come closer than hitting homers in six games in a row. None until Don Mattingly.

On July 18 the fans packed the stands at Arlington Stadium in Texas. People were sitting in the aisles in sticky 94 degree weather. They wanted to see Don tie Dale Long's 31-year-old record.

Jose Guzman pitched for the Rangers. The home crowd moaned as Don grounded out in the first inning. The fans grew quiet as he came to the plate again in the fourth. Guzman pitched carefully and the count went to two balls and no strikes.

The next pitch was an outside fastball. Don reached over and stroked the ball to left center field. Going, going, gone! Don had tied the record. He had hit home runs in eight straight games. The crowd roared and the Yankee first baseman tipped his cap to the fans!

The next day, Don went for the major league record. He grounded out, singled to center, and lined out to first in his first three at-bats. His last chance came in the eighth inning against Ranger reliever Jeff Russell.

The New Yorkers were behind 15–2 as Don stepped into the batter's box. He fouled off the first pitch, then swung and missed. On the next pitch he belted the ball into the left field corner. It stayed inside the ball park for a double.

Don missed breaking the record but the crowd cheered and gave him a standing ovation anyway. Even the Ranger team applauded him from their dugout. During the eight games, Don hit .459 with 21 RBIs.

This home run streak was one of the high points of a tremendous year for the 6' 175-pound athlete. In 1987 Don also blasted six grand slam home runs, setting a new major league record for one season.

The Yankees finished in fourth place in the Eastern Division of the American League with an 89–73 record. Despite back and wrist injuries, Don compiled a .327 batting average. He hit 30 home runs and batted in 115 runs. He was awarded his third Gold Glove after leading the league in fielding. At first base, Don made only five errors in 1,335 total chances.

Donald Arthur Mattingly was born on April 20, 1961, in Evansville, Indiana. He played Little League, Babe Ruth League, and American Legion baseball while growing up.

Don also played baseball, basketball, and football at Evansville Memorial High. In his last two years of high school baseball, he batted .500 and .575.

Though he had several college scholarship offers, Don signed with the Yankees, who selected him in the 19th round of the June, 1979 draft.

In four years of minor league play, his batting average was .332. Don played for Oneonta, New York; Greensboro, North Carolina; Nashville, Tennessee; and Columbus, Ohio before he was promoted to the big leagues in 1983. The young lefthander batted .283 for the Yankees in his rookie season. In 91 games, he had four home runs and 32 RBIs.

1984 was Don's first full season in the majors and it was an outstanding one. He won the American League batting title with a .343 average, the first Yankee to do so since Mickey Mantle in 1956. Don also led the league with 207 hits, 44 doubles, and 55 multi-hit games.

The first baseman came right back in 1985 with a .324 batting average. He blasted 35 home runs and 145 RBIs, scored 107 runs, and got 211 hits. He became the first major leaguer to homer 30 times or more while striking out less than 50 times in a season. To the surprise of no one, Don was named the American League MVP.

The 1986 season convinced many people in the sports world that he was the best player in baseball. His numbers told the story. The talented athlete hit .352 with 31 homers, 113 RBIs, 238 hits (a new Yankee record) and 53 doubles (another Yankee record).

Don became the first American Leaguer ever to get 230 hits, more than 100 RBIs and over 30 home runs in one year. He played in all 162 games and won another Gold Glove.

A New York Times poll of more than 400 major league ballplayers named Don as the best player in the game.

"He's the greatest I've ever seen and he's everything this game should be," said Red Sox hitting coach Walt Hriniak.

After yet another outstanding season in 1987 Don had an off year in 1988. But his off year would still be excellent for any other player in the game. The first baseman batted .311 with 18 home runs, 88 RBIs and 186 hits.

"If he isn't the best, I'd like to know who is," declared Kansas City star and future Hall-of-Famer George Brett. Yet the New York club has never won a division title since Don has worn Yankee pinstripes.

Don stands apart from other players in baseball today. He's a hitter who has a high batting average and also has the power to hit homers and drive in runs. The 28-year-old hardly strikes out and he rarely makes errors in the field. The one thing he can't do is run. Don has only five stolen bases in the last five seasons.

"I think of myself as an everyday player," he explained. "A worker type, consistent over time. Each time I go up to the plate, I want to get a good pitch to hit and hit it hard."

Don and his wife, Kim, have two children.

BATTING CHAMPION Don Mattingly of the New York Yankees cracks his first hit of the 1987 season off a pitch by Detroit Tigers' Dan Petry.

★ KIRBY PUCKETT ★

THE MILWAUKEE BREWERS LED THE MINNESOTA Twins in the sixth inning of the ballgame on August 30, 1987. With the bases loaded, the Brewers were threatening to blow the game wide open.

The Twins needed a win to take over first place in the Western Division. At the plate was the hard-hitting Milwaukee shortstop, Robin Yount.

After fouling off a few pitches, Yount swung hard at a fastball and gave it a ride into deep center field. Kirby Puckett, Twins outfielder, backed up to the warning track. Then with his body against the center field fence and his eye on the ball, he leaped high into the air, glove outstretched.

Although the ball cleared the top of the fence it landed smack into Kirby's glove. He held on to it, robbing Yount of a grand slam. It was the defensive play of the game.

Minnesota came from behind to win the game 10–6. Kirby led the team with six hits and four runs batted in. In addition to his tremendous game-saving catch, he belted two home runs, two doubles, and two singles!

The night before, the 5'8" 210-pound center fielder went four for four with two homers and two singles. His ten hits in two straight nine-inning games set an American League record and tied Rennie Stennett's major league mark.

The two games against the Brewers were typical of the outstanding year Kirby had in 1987. The young slugger batted .332 with 99 RBIs, 28 home runs and 207 hits. He led the Twins in games played (157), at-bats (624), runs scored (96), singles (142), total bases (333), and batting average.

Kirby led the majors with 65 multi-hit games. He tied with Kansas City's Kevin Seitzer for the league lead in hits.

The Twins won their division, the American League pennant, and the World Series in 1987. Kirby was an important reason for their success. He batted .357 in the Series against St. Louis.

He tied Willie McGee for most hits in a Series (10). In one game on October 24, he reached base five times with four singles and a walk (tying another Series record) and scored four runs (still another record).

Kirby Puckett was born March 14, 1961 in Chicago, Illinois. He was the youngest of nine children. The Pucketts lived in a housing project on the south side of the city. It was a tough

40

neighborhood with gangs, crime, and drugs. Kirby's love of baseball kept him out of trouble.

"I'd come home from school, do my homework, then look for kids to play ball with," he recalled. "If nobody played, I'd just throw strikes against the wall or hit rolled-up socks in my room. I loved baseball so much I was always thinking of ways I could keep playing."

Small for his age, Kirby was short and skinny when he entered high school. "I decided if I was going to be short, I was going to be strong," he explained.

Kirby became a body builder and began lifting weights. He grew only to 5'8" but he added enough muscle to bench press 350 pounds. Today he's called "the strongest little man in baseball."

At Calumet High School Kirby earned All-America honors. The pro scouts thought he was too short and Kirby wasn't offered a contract from any team. After high school graduation he went to work at the local Ford car plant.

The following summer Kirby traveled to the Kansas City Royals free agent tryouts. He didn't make the team, but Coach Dewey Kalmer offered him a scholarship to attend Bradley University in Peoria, Illinois. Kirby played center field well enough to make the All-Missouri Valley Conference team in 1981.

When his father died, Kirby transferred to Triton Community College in River Grove, Illinois to be near his mother. In his one season at Triton, the 21-year-old hit .472 with 16 home runs and 42 stolen bases. Pro teams noticed his success and the Twins drafted him on January, 1982 as a free agent.

In the minor leagues, the young athlete batted .382 for Elizabethton, Tennessee and .314 for Visalia, California. He stole many bases but hit few home runs. After starting 1984 with AAA Toledo, Kirby was brought up to the Twins to bat in the leadoff spot.

In his first big league game, he got four hits. He batted .296 in his rookie season with 165 hits and 31 RBIs. His job was to get on base even if it meant sacrificing home run power.

In 1985 Kirby batted .288 with 199 hits. He improved his RBI total to 74 and hit four home runs. During the offseason he worked with Twins batting coach Tony Oliva, who taught him to hit to all fields with power.

Kirby exploded in 1986. In the month of April alone he hit eight home runs, doubling his previous big league total. His work with Oliva paid off. He proved he could hit homers as well as singles. He batted .328 in 1986 with 223 hits, 31 home runs, and 96 RBIs. He led the Twins in stolen bases (20) and won his first Gold Glove.

"What you've got now is the complete ballplayer," said Dodgers manager Tommy Lasorda. "Speed, defense, arm, power, average. Plus he's a great human being."

After his outstanding 1987 season when the Twins became world champions, Kirby recorded another tremendous year in 1988. Now third in the batting order, he hit .356 (second in the major leagues).

For the third season in a row, he collected over 200 hits. Kirby's total of 234 led both leagues. He also hit 24 home runs and batted in

121 runs (first in the majors). The Twins, with a 91–71 record, finished second in the West behind Oakland.

"I love the game of baseball," declared the 28-year-old. "I have so much fun at it."

Kirby and his wife, Tonya, live in Minnesota.

GO AHEAD, MAKE MY DAY: Minnesota Twins'
Kirby Puckett blasts one for a homer.

★ MIKE SCHMIDT ★

Sports fans everywhere followed the ball game on April 18, 1987. They wanted to know if Mike Schmidt, one of the greatest sluggers in baseball, would hit his 500th home run.

The Philadelphia Phillies were playing the Pirates in Pittsburgh. Bucs pitcher Don Robinson had a one-run lead in the bottom of the ninth inning. There were two outs and one man on base.

Third baseman Mike Schmidt knew the game was on the line as he stepped to the plate. Robinson studied his catcher's signs. He nodded his head and pitched the ball. What happened next is history.

"Schmidt swings. It's a high drive, deep to center field. It's going, going, that ball is out of here!" screamed the excited announcer. "Mike Schmidt has won the game for Philadelphia by

45

hitting his 500th home run! The Pittsburgh fans are giving him a standing ovation!" It was the perfect moment for Mike to become the 14th player in baseball history to hit 500 homers.

The Michael Jack Schmidt story starts in Dayton, Ohio where he was born on September 27, 1949. Mike loved all sports. As a little boy of four or five he first played baseball with a plastic Whiffle ball. Then he joined Little League when he was eight.

At Fairview High School, Mike played baseball, football, and basketball. But he hurt his knees playing football and had to have surgery on them. Mike once said, "Sports was the only thing that mattered to me."

In 1967, Mike started college at Ohio University. He studied architecture and business. He also played baseball on the freshman team as a shortstop.

Mike did well, moving up to the varsity to become the star of the team. He was named a college All-American twice and played in the College World Series in 1970.

June, 1971 was a good month for Mike. He graduated from Ohio University with a degree in business administration and was selected in the second round of the baseball draft by the Philadelphia Phillies.

Mike was assigned to Reading, Pennsylvania, the Phillies' AA team. There, he played in 74 games and batted .211. Then he was promoted to the Phillies' AAA club in Eugene, Oregon. Mike played in 131 games and batted .291. He had 26 home runs and 91 RBIs. He was named the Pacific Coast League's All-Star second baseman.

After Eugene lost to Albuquerque 3–1 in the league playoffs, the Phillies called up three players. Catcher Bob Boone, shortstop Craig Robinson, and second baseman Mike Schmidt were asked to join the team in Philadelphia and play in the major leagues.

Mike signed with the Phillies on September 12 and was in the lineup that night against the Mets. The starting third baseman was Don Money. He left after two innings with a bad back. Mike took over at third base and has played there ever since.

During his rookie year with the Phillies in 1972, Mike hit .192 with just 18 homers. But he didn't give up, and in 1973 he made a strong comeback, hitting .282 with 36 home runs. After that, he never looked back.

His 100th homer was on April 20, 1976. Just three days earlier, Mike belted four homers in one game at Wrigley Field in Chicago. He hit four straight home runs again in July, 1979.

Mike's 300th homer came in New York in August, 1981. His 400th homer was in May, 1984, against the Los Angeles Dodgers.

Mike has always tried to be a good all-around player. His excellent defensive play at third base has earned him ten Gold Glove Awards in his 17-year career. He led the National League in home runs during eight seasons and was selected to the All-Star Game 11 times.

The 6'2" 203 pound athlete is a three-time MVP in the National League. He won it first in 1980 when he led the Phillies to their first-ever World Championship. Mike was chosen the Series MVP after getting eight hits and seven RBIs.

He was League MVP in 1981 and again in 1986. Only two others, Stan Musial and Roy Campanella, have ever been three-time winners in the National League.

Named the "Greatest Phillies Player Ever," Mike relaxes by playing golf. The future Hall-of-Famer believes that the key to success in baseball is "to hit .280 or .290, drive in 120 runs, and still hit 30 to 35 home runs."

In 1987, the talented infielder hit .293, had 113 RBIs and swatted 35 home runs. A shoulder injury caused Mike to miss one-third of the 1988 season. But he still managed to hit 12 home runs and knock in 62 RBIs for the Phillies.

After a successful operation in the off-season, Mike returned to the Philadelphia lineup in 1989. However his performance didn't meet his own high standards. Two months into the season, Mike had hit six home runs, collected 28 RBIs, but batted only .203. On May 29, 1989, the 39-year-old man, who many consider to be the best third baseman to ever play the game, retired from baseball.

Mike hit a total of 548 home runs in his career. That puts him seventh on the all-time list. Only Reggie Jackson (563), Harmon Killebrew (573), Frank Robinson (586), Willie Mays (660), the great Babe Ruth (714) and the incomparable Hank Aaron (755) are ranked higher.

"I never look at myself as a hero," he once said. "I look at myself as someone surrounded by blessings. In exchange, I try to stay active in community projects and create a good example.

"If a kid has a Mike Schmidt poster in his bedroom, I want his parents to be happy about it," he added.

Mike is married. He and his wife, Donna, have two children.

AND IT'S A GOOD ONE! Philadelphia Phillies' Mike Schmidt watches home run number 528— his 33rd of the 1987 season—as it leaves the ballpark.

★ DARRYL STRAWBERRY ★

It was the summer of 1985. New York Mets slugger Darryl Strawberry was as hot as the weather in Chicago on the afternoon of August 5.

Early in the season, the young ballplayer tore a ligament in his right thumb while making a diving catch. The injury required immediate surgery, and Darryl was placed on the disabled list. He missed seven weeks of the season.

Back in the lineup after June 28, the 23-year-old started tearing the league apart. The Mets were making a run for the division title. Just two weeks earlier, Darryl had singlehandedly destroyed the Atlanta Braves. He hit two home runs, one of which was a grand slam.

He also slugged a triple and batted in seven runs in the 16–4 Met victory. No Met had collected seven RBIs in a game since Dave Kingman knocked in eight runs in 1976 against the Dodgers.

Now with a win at Wrigley Field, the New Yorkers could move into first place, ahead of the St. Louis Cardinals. 34,167 fans watched as Cub rookie pitcher Derek Botelho walked Keith Hernandez and Gary Carter. It was the first inning and there were two outs.

Darryl stepped into the batter's box. With the count two balls and two strikes, he smacked an outside fastball into the right field bleachers for a three-run homer.

Two innings later Botelho faced the powerful outfielder again with two outs. This time the count went to 1 and 2. Darryl made contact on the next pitch and belted a tremendous home run into the seats in center field. The Mets led by four runs.

Darryl was intentionally walked in the fifth inning. In the seventh he faced Cub reliever Ron Meredith with two outs. The lefthander delivered a fastball to the plate and Darryl whacked the first pitch over the fence for his third home run of the game.

The talented slugger also singled (for his second career four-hit game) and tied a Met record with 13 total bases. Darryl had five RBIs and scored four runs as the Mets beat the Cubs 7–2.

New York took over first place in the Eastern Division that afternoon. They lost the title in the last few days of the season to the St. Louis Cardinals. The Mets finished in second place with a 98–64 record, three games back.

In 1985 Darryl set a club record for left-handed hitters by slugging 29 home runs. He

52

batted .277 with 79 RBIs despite missing more than 50 games because of his thumb injury.

Darryl Strawberry was born on March 12, 1962 in Los Angeles, California. He played baseball and basketball as a child and did well in both sports.

At Crenshaw High School in Los Angeles, Darryl helped his team win the city championship in basketball. As a ballplayer he hit .371 in his junior year and batted .400 in his senior year.

Darryl had many scholarship offers from colleges in both sports. He chose baseball and was the number-one draft choice in the country in 1980. The talented athlete signed with New York after high school graduation. He played for Kingsport, Tennessee, the Mets' Rookie team in the Appalachian League. In his first professional at-bat he singled to center.

At the Lynchburg, Virginia A club in 1981, he hit 13 home runs and stole 31 bases. Playing AA ball at Jackson, Mississippi in 1982, he was the Texas League's MVP. Darryl batted .283 with 123 hits, 34 home runs, 97 RBIs, and 45 stolen bases.

He was promoted to the Mets AAA club in Tidewater, Virginia in 1983. After 16 games (in which the young outfielder collected 19 hits and 7 stolen bases) he was moved up to the major leagues.

In his first season with the Mets, the 21-year-old hit .257 with 26 home runs, 74 RBIs and 108 hits. He was named Rookie of the Year.

In 1984 the second-year player led the club in homers and RBIs (97). He became only the second 20/20 man in Mets history with 26 homers and 27 steals.

After an outstanding season in 1985, Darryl came right back in '86 to help lead the Mets to a World Series victory over the Red Sox. His 123 hits, including 27 home runs, 93 RBIs and 28 stolen bases, contributed to the team's 108 wins during the regular season.

In 1987 Darryl recorded the best numbers of his major league career. The Mets didn't repeat as world champions. They finished second in the East. But the 6'6" 190-pound outfielder broke the 30/30 barrier with 39 home runs and 36 stolen bases.

Darryl set Mets records in runs (108), home runs, and extra base hits (76). He batted .284, a career high, with 104 RBIs and 151 hits (another personal high).

The Mets came back in 1988 to take first place in the National League East with 100 wins and 60 losses. Darryl was in the thick of it all season long. He belted 39 homers (first in the league), batted in 101 runs (second in the league) and scored 101 runs (fourth in the league). The Mets lost in the seventh game of the League Championship Series to Los Angeles.

Tall and slim, Darryl's power comes from his arms, hands, and wrists. After six years in the big leagues, many feel he's just beginning to reach his peak.

"If I could pick one guy in all of baseball to start an expansion team with," said Whitey Herzog, manager of the Cardinals, "it'd have to be Strawberry. Strawberry's the guy!"

Darryl is married. He and his wife, Lisa, have two children.

IN LIKE FLYNN: New York Mets' Darryl Strawberry slides safely into home to score against the St. Louis Cardinals.

★ HANK AARON ★

I**T WAS THE BIGGEST CROWD IN** A**TLANTA** S**TADIUM** since the Braves moved from Milwaukee nine years earlier. 53,775 people watched balloons and fireworks before the game.

Among the spectators was Governor Jimmy Carter of Georgia and Mayor Maynard Jackson of Atlanta. Broadcasters and writers from all over the world, along with a national television audience, waited to watch the Braves play the Dodgers. It was the rainy night of April 8, 1974.

They were all gathered together to witness baseball history. Right fielder Henry Aaron of the Atlanta Braves had hit his 714th home run on the first swing of the bat in the season opener only four days before. That tied Hank with Babe Ruth, 39 years after the famous "Sultan of Swat" set the major league record for round-trippers.

The home crowd in Atlanta was hoping to see "Hammerin' Hank" belt his 715th homer to break the record which many thought would last forever.

The first time up, Hank walked without ever getting the bat off his shoulder. Al Downing, the Dodgers pitcher, was taking no chances with the famous slugger.

Rain was falling steadily by the fourth inning. The Dodgers were ahead 3–1. Darrell Evans led off for the Braves with a hot grounder that shortstop Bill Russell couldn't handle. Evans was on first as Hank came to the plate. The crowd roared their encouragement.

Downing's first pitch was inside for ball one. On the second pitch, Hank swung and smacked it solidly. The ball rose high in the air toward left-center field. The fans jumped to their feet screaming. It traveled over the outfield fence, 385 feet away into the Atlanta bullpen. A home run!

Relief pitcher Tom House made a one-handed catch of the valuable baseball. Fireworks lit up the sky and the scoreboard flashed "715" in big numbers. As the crowd gave him a standing ovation, Hank Aaron slowly circled the bases, enjoying the moment. His teammates stood at home plate ready to congratulate the 40-year-old star.

Tom House gave Hank the ball, and he also received a plaque from the Braves' owner. Atlanta went on to win the game, beating the Dodgers 7–4. Later in the clubhouse, his teammates drank a champagne toast to Henry Louis Aaron, the greatest all-time home run hitter in baseball history!

He was born February 5, 1934 in Mobile, Alabama, one of eight children in the Herbert Aaron family. Hank played softball in the city playground leagues because there were no organized baseball teams at school. When he was a teenager in 1947, Jackie Robinson became the first black baseball player in the major leagues. He became Hank's hero and role model.

At Central High School and Josephine Allen Institute in Mobile, he played on the football team and was a star halfback and end. He was offered a scholarship to play college football at Florida A & M but he turned it down.

A scout from the local black semi-pro baseball team was impressed by Hank's play in softball and signed him up. While still in high school, the 16-year-old teenager played baseball on Sundays for the Mobile Black Bears.

The Bears played the Indianapolis Clowns, another black team, and they took notice of the talented young ballplayer. The following spring, Hank was mailed a contract to play full-time for the Clowns in Indianapolis.

Hank played shortstop and was an outstanding hitter, leading the Negro American League with a .467 batting average. A couple of major league clubs were impressed by Henry and offered him contracts. He decided to sign with the Braves and play with their minor league club at Eau Claire, Wisconsin in the Northern League. In 1952, Hank was named to the Northern League All-Star team and was voted Rookie of the Year with a .336 average.

The following year, the 18-year-old played second base for another Braves minor league club, the Jacksonville Tars of the South Atlantic

League in Florida. Henry helped lead the team to the League Championship and was named Most Valuable Player during the 1953 season. He batted .362, had 208 hits, and 125 RBIs.

The Braves sent Hank to play winter ball in Puerto Rico and decided to play him in the outfield. He was scheduled to start the 1954 season with the minor league AAA Toledo club, when Braves outfielder Bobby Thomson broke his ankle in March. Hank was picked to replace Thomson in left field. He had finally made it to the major leagues!

In his rookie season, Hank batted .280 with 69 RBIs and 13 home runs. It was a good beginning for the 20-year-old, who broke his ankle on September 5 and missed the last few weeks of the season.

By his second year, Hank began to show the numbers that would make him a respected and feared hitter over the next twenty-one years. He hit .314, belted 27 home runs and drove in 106 RBIs.

From 1955 through 1974, Hank had 20 or more home runs each year. He had 30 or more home runs in 15 seasons. He batted in more than 100 runs in 11 different seasons. In 1963 alone, he hit 44 homers, had 130 RBIs and stole 31 bases, a rare combination of speed and power.

One of his most memorable moments came on September 23, 1957. The Braves were playing the Cardinals for the National League pennant, and the score was tied 2–2 in the bottom of the 11th inning.

"Precisely at 11:34, twenty-six minutes before midnight," recalled Hank, "I hit a pitch over the center field fence with a runner on base and we beat St. Louis 4–2." It was his 44th home run in a year that saw him hit .322 with 132 RBIs.

The city of Milwaukee went wild with excitement. Hank led the Braves to the world championship by beating the Yankees four games to three. "Hammerin' Hank" batted .393 in the World Series. He had 11 hits, seven RBIs, one triple and three home runs!

The Braves faced the Yankees in the Series again in 1958, but lost to the New Yorkers in seven games. In 1969 Atlanta finished first in the Western Division, but lost the pennant to the Eastern Division New York Mets in the National League Championship Series.

Hank retired at the end of the 1976 season after 23 years in the major leagues. He was 42 years old. He spent his last two years back in Milwaukee, playing for the American League Brewers.

The 6′ 190-pound athlete was the first player in baseball history with 3,000 career hits and more than 500 homers. He batted .305 lifetime, drove in a record 2,297 runs, and had 3,771 hits.

Hank hit his 100th homer in August, 1957. Sixteen years later, he hit his 700th home run in July of 1973. During his career, he slugged a total of 755 home runs. He appeared in 24 All-Star Games, and won many awards and honors during his career.

"Giving your job the best you've got—that's the only way you are going to be successful," he declared, "no matter whether you are playing baseball or delivering mail."

Hank Aaron was elected to the Baseball Hall of Fame in 1982. He is married and has four children.

THREE THOUSAND AND COUNTING: *Atlanta Braves outfielder Hank Aaron makes the 3000th hit of his career during a 1970 game against the Cincinnati Reds. He was ninth man in the history of baseball to break the 3000-hit mark, and went on to collect baseball's all-time record for home runs, beating Babe Ruth's total of 714.*

★ JOE DiMAGGIO ★

THE LARGEST CROWD EVER ASSEMBLED TO SEE A game of night baseball in the major leagues was in Cleveland Stadium on July 17, 1941. They were there to see one man—Joltin' Joe Di-Maggio of the New York Yankees. Many called him the Yankee Clipper because his style and grace were similar to the tall sailing ships of the past.

Joe had accomplished one of the greatest baseball feats of all time. He had hit safely in 56 straight ball games! Everyone asked the same question, "Could the amazing streak continue?"

It all started with a single on May 15 against the Chicago White Sox at Yankee Stadium. No one took notice at first. After Joe hit in twenty straight games, the players and writers began to pay attention.

The Yankee record for a hitting streak was 29

games. In game 30, which would break the record, Joe hit a ground ball to the shortstop. It
took a bad hop and bounced off his shoulder.
Everybody waited to see the scorer's decision.
Was it a hit or an error? The scorer signaled
"hit" and the streak stayed alive.

On June 29, against the Washington Senators,
Joe broke the modern American League record
of 41 games. It was set in 1922 by George Sisler
of the St. Louis Browns. Then he broke the all-
time major league record set by Wee Willie Keeler in 1897. Keeler hit safely in 44 straight
games. In game 45 Joe's hit against the Boston
Red Sox was a home run.

Each day, Americans asked, "Did DiMaggio
get a hit? Is the streak still alive?" And each
day, Joe came through—from home runs to singles hit slowly down the line.

In game 47 against the Athletics, he swatted
three singles and a double. In game 50 against
the Browns, the famous Yankee got three singles and a home run. In game 56 against the In-
dians Joe clugged a double and two singles
During the hitting streak, his batting average
was a sizzling .408!

Joe faced a Cleveland lefthander, Al Smith, in
game 57. His first time up, the Yankee Clipper
smashed the ball down the third base line. Infielder Ken Keltner reached over, grabbed the
ball, and made the long throw to first for the
out.

Next time at bat, Joe walked. Later he swatted
another hot grounder to the third baseman.
Keltner robbed him of a hit with a sensational
stop and an accurate throw to first.

In the eighth inning, Joe came up for the last

time. The streak was on the line. The bases were loaded with only one out. Cleveland reliever Jim Bagby, Jr. faced the famous athlete. With the count one ball and one strike, Joe hit a bad-hop grounder to shortstop Lou Boudreau, who turned it into a double play.

The Yankees won the game, 4–3, but Joltin' Joe's streak was over. He set a major league record which many believe will never be broken!

The next day, Joe began another hitting streak, but it lasted for only 16 games. 1941 was a tremendous year for the Yankee center fielder. He hit .357, with 30 home runs and 43 doubles. He also led the league with 125 runs batted in and was voted the MVP. The Yankees went to the World Series where they beat the Brooklyn Dodgers in five games for the championship.

Joseph Paul DiMaggio was born in Martinez, California on November 25, 1914. He was one of eight children. Joe's parents were Italian immigrants and his father was a fisherman in San Francisco.

Joe had always been good at baseball ever since he began playing at age ten. The kids played in a vacant lot, used rocks for bases, and an oar handle as a bat. Most played without gloves and the ball was often repaired with bicycle tape.

Young Joe played the infield and was the best player in the neighborhood. He was a member of the Francisco Junior High team and also played street football and tennis. When he was 14, Joe played for the Boy's Club League and led them to a championship.

Never a good student, the shy teenager quit Galileo High School in 1931 when he was 17. He worked full-time and played on semi-pro baseball teams. Joe performed so well that local minor league teams took an interest in him.

The 6′2″ 18-year-old tried out for the San Francisco Seals of the Pacific Coast League. Joe's older brother, Vince, was a member of the team. The young athlete played the last few games of the 1932 season for the Seals and belted a triple his first time at bat. Joe started the 1933 season on the bench but began playing the outfield after several weeks.

From the very beginning, Joe played well and became a favorite with the fans. As a right fielder for the Seals, he hit .340 in 1933 with 28 home runs, 45 doubles, 13 triples and 169 RBIs. Early in the season he began a hitting streak which lasted 61 straight games. 19-year-old Joe became the best known player in minor league baseball that year.

In 1934 he had another great season, hitting .341 with 18 doubles, 6 triples, 12 home runs, and 69 RBIs. Several major league clubs were interested in purchasing Joe's contract, but a knee injury scared them off.

Joe's 1935 season with the Seals convinced the Yankees he was major league material. He hit .398 with 34 roundtrippers and 24 stolen bases. The 21-year-old was voted the Pacific Coast League MVP.

Joe headed for New York City and was thrust into the public eye immediately. Some said he might be the next Babe Ruth. A foot injury prevented him from playing on opening day in 1936.

His debut came on May 3. The young rookie connected for a triple and two singles as the Yankees beat the Browns 14–5. Joe lived up to

65

all the publicity written about him that year. He had an outstanding season and was named the Rookie of the Year. He batted .323, slugged 29 home runs, and drove in 125 runs.

The Yankees went to the World Series and beat the New York Giants in six games. Joe hit .346, his career high for World Series play, and made a spectacular catch in center field.

Joltin' Joe played with the Yankees for 13 seasons. (From 1943 to 1945 he was in the Army Air Force and didn't play pro baseball.) His batting average was over .300 in all but two seasons. The two-time batting champ was named the Most Valuable Player three times (1939, 1941, and 1947). The Yankees won nine World Series and ten American League pennants during those 13 years.

Up until 1941, Joe was a great baseball star. After his 56-game hitting streak, he became a living legend!

During his career Joe hit 361 home runs and had a .325 lifetime batting average. He collected 2,214 hits and drove in 1,537 RBIs. Bothered by injuries in his last few seasons, Joltin' Joe retired in 1951 at the age of 37. In 1969 he was named the Greatest Living Player by sportswriters.

"What I will remember most in days to come," he declared in 1951, "will be the great loyalty of the fans. They have been very good to me."

Joe was elected to the Baseball Hall of Fame in 1955. He has one child.

JOLTIN' JOE DiMaggio hammers out a hit in a 1941 game against the hapless Washington Senators. DiMaggio led the league in RBIs that year with 125.

★ JACKIE ROBINSON ★

APRIL 18, 1946 WAS OPENING DAY IN THE INTERnational Baseball League. The New Jersey Giants were playing the Montreal Royals at Roosevelt Stadium in Jersey City. The Royals were the Brooklyn Dodgers' top minor league club, just one step below the major leagues.

This game marked the debut of 26-year-old Jackie Robinson. He was specially picked by Dodger President Branch Rickey to be the first black man to play in organized professional baseball.

There were separate negro baseball leagues and Jackie had played one year for an all-black team called the Kansas City Monarchs. But this was the white professional leagues and 52,000 fans waited to see the drama unfold.

Jackie's knees felt shaky and his hands were sweating as he came to bat in the first inning.

With a three and two count, he hit a bouncing ball to the shortstop, who threw him out at first.

Jackie came to bat again in the third inning with two men on base. The Giants expected him to bunt but the talented athlete slugged a letter-high fastball over the left field fence, 330 feet away. It was a three-run homer!

In the fifth inning, the Royals led 6–0. Jackie bunted and beat the throw to first for an infield hit. Then he stole second and advanced to third on a fielder's choice.

The crowd roared as Jackie took a long lead off third and scampered back when the pitcher threw over. Again, he took a long lead, but this time the Giant pitcher stopped in the middle of his delivery. The umpire called a balk and Jackie scored.

He singled in the seventh. In the eighth he bunted safely again and scored on another balk by the pitcher. The Royals won the game 14–1. Jackie had four hits, scored four times, drove in three runs, and stole two bases.

Many had questioned if a black man could be good enough to play professional baseball. Jackie's performance that day and the rest of the season quieted everyone's doubts.

Throughout the year he faced insults and name-calling from fans and other ballplayers because he was black. Jackie kept his anger to himself. Instead, he took out his frustrations on the ball.

He led the International League in hitting with a .349 average and in runs scored with 113. He finished second in stolen bases and drove in 66 runs. He also had the highest fielding percentage of any second baseman.

Traveling with the team, Jackie couldn't eat in the same restaurants or sleep in the same hotels as his teammates. It was worse in the South. There were even separate bathrooms and drinking fountains for whites and blacks.

The Montreal Royals won the league title in 1946. They played the Louisville Colonels in the Little World Series. The first three games were played in Kentucky and Jackie was booed every time he came to the plate by the nearly all-white crowd. Many black spectators were turned away.

The Royals lost two of the three games in Louisville and Jackie got only one hit. When the team returned to Montreal, Canada, they won three straight and became Little World Series Champions.

Jackie scored the game-winning run in one game, and had a double, triple and a bases-loaded squeeze bunt in another. He was a hero in Montreal.

During spring training before the 1947 season, on the morning of April 9, Dodger President Branch Rickey distributed a press release. It said, "Brooklyn announces the purchase of the contract of Jack Roosevelt Robinson from Montreal."

Jackie was now an official member of the Brooklyn Dodgers and the first black man to play in the major leagues in modern times. (Moses Walker once played for the American Association in 1884.)

On April 15, 1947, the Dodgers opened their regular season against the Milwaukee Braves at Ebbets Field in New York. Jackie started the game at first base. He went hitless that afternoon in a game that had little excitement. But it marked the beginning of a new era in professional baseball and eventually all pro sports. Jack Roosevelt Robinson had broken the color line in America's favorite pastime!

He was born on January 31, 1919 in Cairo, Georgia, one of five children. The family moved to Southern California when Jackie was still a toddler and he grew up in Pasadena.

"Sports had been a big thing with me since I was a little boy," explained Jackie.

At John Muir Technical High School in Pasadena, he was a standout in football, basketball, baseball, and track. At Pasadena Junior College he played quarterback for the school football team and shortstop for the championship baseball team. He also broke track and field records in broad jumping.

Jackie got a scholarship and transferred to UCLA after two years. He was considered the most outstanding all-around athlete in the country. In basketball he twice led the Pacific Coast Conference in scoring, and he averaged 11 yards per carry in football. He was National Collegiate Athletic Association (NCAA) champion in the broad jump.

He won the Pacific Coast Intercollegiate golf championship, several swimming titles, and was also an excellent tennis player.

During his senior year, Jackie dropped out of school to find a job and support his family. He worked as a coach and played for a football team called the Los Angeles Bulldogs.

Drafted into the Army in 1942, Jackie went to Officer's Candidate School and was discharged in November, 1944 as a lieutenant. In 1945 he joined the Kansas City Monarchs baseball club. That's when Branch Rickey decided this educated and talented athlete would be the perfect person to break the color barrier in professional baseball.

Jackie's first year in a Brooklyn Dodgers uniform was a difficult one. He was the object of horrible insults and threats on his life. But his excellent play and quiet dignity captured the admiration of everyone.

The Dodgers came in first in the National League with a 94–60 record. Jackie batted .297, scored 125 runs, and had 175 hits. He slugged 12 homers, drove in 48 runs and led the league in stolen bases.

By the time Brooklyn met the Yankees in the World Series, Jackie was an accepted part of the team. He had seven hits and batted .259 in the Series as the Yankees beat the Dodgers four games to three.

Jackie played for Brooklyn for ten seasons. His lifetime batting average was .311 with 137 home runs, 197 stolen bases, 734 RBIs and 1,518 hits. He was voted the National League MVP in 1949 when he hit .342 and drove in 124 runs.

When the 5'11½" 195-pound athlete retired after the 1956 season, all but three major league baseball clubs had black players on their teams. Jackie went on to be an outspoken supporter of civil rights for black Americans until his death on October 24, 1972 at the age of 53.

"A life is not important except in the impact it has on other lives," he once said. "I still feel I owe—until every child can have an equal opportunity; until hunger is illegal; until hatred is recognized as a disease and treated as such, and until racism and drugs are conquered."

Jackie Robinson was elected to the Pro Baseball Hall of Fame in 1962. He and his wife, Rachel, had four children.

DA BUMS! Dodgers Jackie Robinson (right) and Gil Hodges (left) reenact their bizarre home-plate play in a game against the Chicago Cubs in 1950. Robinson was on third and Hodges on second when teammate Eddie Miksis blooped a high rounder to third. Bob Ramazzotti fielded the hit and pegged it to Cubs catcher Mickey Owen; Robinson turned back, only to find Hodges on third base. When Owen saw Miksis heading past first base he threw to Cubs second baseman Wayne (Twig) Terwilliger, and Robinson and Hodges both streaked for home. They arrived in a photo finish, only to be tagged out. Brooklyn won anyway, 6–1.

★ TED WILLIAMS ★

THEY CALLED HIM "THE KID" AND "THE SPLENDID Splinter." 23-year-old Ted Williams of the Boston Red Sox was one of baseball's biggest stars in 1941. The slim, 6'3" outfielder had been hammering American League pitchers all season long.

It wasn't until the last week of the season that Ted's batting average fell below .400. With two games left to play against the Philadelphia Athletics, his average had dipped to .39955.

"Will he finish over .400?" the fans and sportswriters asked one another.

No one had come close to that magic number since Bill Terry hit .401 for the New York Giants of the National League in 1930.

"Do you want to play in those last two games or sit them out, Ted?" asked Red Sox manager, Joe Cronin. If Ted didn't get a few hits against

Philadelphia, Cronin knew his average would drop quickly.

"I'm playing, Joe," answered Ted instantly. "If I'm going to be a .400 hitter, I'm not going to slip in through the back door."

The Sunday doubleheader was at Shibe Park in Philadelphia. It was a cold, wet, and muddy field. Ted took special batting practice that morning. When he came to the plate for the first time he was warmed up and ready.

Dick Fowler was pitching for the A's. He wound up and threw one over the plate. Ted belted a liner into right field for a clean single. The fans cheered loudly. His average was above .400. But could he keep hitting?

When Ted walked to the plate for the second time, the fans quieted down. Fowler threw a fast ball down the middle.

"Strike one!" yelled the umpire.

The second pitch was another fast ball. This time, the "Splendid Splinter" blasted it over the right field wall and across the street for his 37th home run!

Ted got two more hits that game and was four for five. His average was safely above .400. No one expected the young slugger to play the second game.

Ted refused to sit on the bench. When he came to the plate, the fans gave him a standing ovation. "The Kid" answered the applause with a ground single to right.

In the fourth inning, Ted blasted a line drive directly into one of the loud speakers on the right field wall. The speaker was badly dented. The ball bounced back onto the field for a ground rule double. The fans had never seen such a hard-hit ball.

The game was finally called because of darkness. Ted had gotten six hits in eight times at bat. His final batting average was .406. He had made baseball history.

In 1941, Ted Williams had 37 home runs, 120 runs batted in, and 185 hits. He was the first player in 11 years to hit over .400. He was also the last player to do it. Since 1941, only a few ballplayers have even come close.

Theodore Samuel Williams was born on August 30, 1918 in San Diego, California. As a young boy he loved baseball. He once told his mother, "I'm going to be like Babe Ruth when I grow up."

Ted played ball whenever he could with the other kids. He began to develop into a strong hitter with a powerful swing. He played on his junior high and high school teams.

During his last two years at Herbert Hoover High School, Ted hit .586 and .403. By the age of 17, major league scouts had noticed the young athlete.

The teenager was offered a contract with the New York Yankees, but his mother wanted him to stay close to home. Ted soon signed with the local minor league team, the San Diego Padres. After two years with the Padres, the Boston Red Sox bought his contract.

Nineteen-year-old Ted was sent to Boston's AAA farm club, the Minneapolis Millers. Although he was a good hitter he needed work on his fielding.

Ted had a terrific year with the Millers. He

batted .366, drove in 142 runs and smacked 43 home runs. Even his fielding improved.

Ted was promoted to Boston for the 1939 season. In his rookie year he hit .327 with 31 homers and 145 RBIs. The "Splinter" raised his average to .344 in 1940 followed by his incredible .406 in 1941.

He was already a great star in Boston. At the 1941 All-Star Game, Ted became a hero to sports fans everywhere. The National League led the American League 5–4 in the bottom of the ninth inning. With two outs and two men on base "The Kid" smacked a high fast ball into the right field seats for a home run. The American League won the game 7–5.

After batting .356 in 1942 Ted left baseball to go into the service. America was involved in World War II. The famous slugger joined the Marines and became a pilot.

Lieutenant Williams served his country for more than three years. When he reported back to the Red Sox in 1946, he was 27 years old. Were his best days in baseball behind him? That was the question on everyone's mind.

Ted now weighed 180 pounds. No longer the skinny kid, he quickly took over where he had left off. His performance in the 1946 All-Star Game has been called the greatest in its history. He belted two home runs and two singles, batted in five runs and scored four runs.

Ted had such a hot bat that year that Lou Boudreau, player-manager of Cleveland, came up with an idea. He shifted his fielders toward right field where Ted usually hit the ball. Soon, other ballclubs did the same. Every time Ted came to the plate, players used the Boudreau

Shift. He could have gotten hits by slapping the ball into left field but Ted wouldn't back down from the challenge.

"I'll hammer the ball into right field anyway," he declared, and he did. Even the Boudreau Shift couldn't stop the Boston slugger.

Ted finished 1946 with a .342 average and was named the League's Most Valuable Player. The Red Sox finally won the American League pennant.

Ted badly bruised his elbow in an exhibition game and batted only .200 in the World Series. He got only five singles as the Red Sox lost to the St. Louis Cardinals.

From 1947 through 1951, Ted batted above .300 every year. His .343 average, 43 homers and 159 RBIs earned him the MVP award in 1949.

In 1952, with the Korean War still on, Ted was called back into the Marines. He flew 39 missions as a combat pilot and won three medals.

Ted reported back to the Red Sox at the end of the 1953 season. In just 37 games, he collected 37 hits including 13 home runs. At the age of 34, the "Splendid Splinter" was still one of the greatest hitters in baseball!

Ted played for Boston through the 1960 season, but the Red Sox never won another pennant. In the six years after his return from Korea he led the league in hitting four times. He was the oldest player ever to win a batting title at age 40 in 1958.

In 19 seasons, his lifetime batting average was .344. He had a total of 2,654 hits, 521 home runs and 1,839 RBIs.

Ted managed the Washington Senators from 1969 to 1971 and the Texas Rangers in 1972. He was a batting instructor for the Red Sox and is an expert fisherman.

Ted's final game was on September 26, 1960. He stood at home plate for the last time in the eighth inning. The fans gave him a thunderous standing ovation.

On the first pitch, Ted took a ball. Then he swung at a high slider. With the count one ball and one strike the next pitch was a waist-high fast ball on the outside corner.

Ted swung and his bat made contact. The ball rose in the air and headed into center field and over the bullpen fence. The fans screamed themselves hoarse. He had ended his career with a tremendous home run!

Ted Williams was voted into the Baseball Hall of Fame in 1966. He has two children.

FOUR-HUNDRED-NINETY-NINE AND DEFI-
NITELY COUNTING: *Boston Red Sox slugger
Ted Williams sends his 499th home run winging
its way into the stands in the ninth inning of a
1960 Detroit-Boston game.*

BIBLIOGRAPHY

BOOKS

Aaron, Henry, as told to Bisher, Furman. *AARON, R. F.* New York: The World Publishing Company, 1968.

Baldwin, Stan, and Jenkins, Jerry, in collaboration with Hank Aaron. *BAD HENRY*. Radnor, Pennsylvania: Chilton Book Company, 1974.

DeGregorio, George. *JOE DiMAGGIO—AN INFORMAL BIOGRAPHY*. New York: Stein and Day, 1981.

Durfee, Dan. *BASEBALL'S BIG SIX*. Worthington, Ohio: Willowisp Press, 1987.

Herbert, Mike. *MIKE SCHMIDT—THE HUMAN VACUUM CLEANER*. Chicago: Children's Press, 1982.

Hochman, Stan. *MIKE SCHMIDT—BASEBALL'S KING OF SWING*. New York: Random House, 1983.

Linn, Ed. *TED WILLIAMS—THE ETERNAL KID*. New York: Thomas Nelson & Sons, 1961.

Liss, Howard. *TRIPLE CROWN WINNERS*. New York: Julian Messner, 1969.

Moore, Jack B. *JOE DiMAGGIO—A BIO-BIBLIOGRAPHY*. New York: Greenwood Press, 1986.

Robinson, Jackie, as told to Duckett, Alfred. *I NEVER HAD IT MADE*. New York: G.P. Putnam's Sons, 1972.

Schlossberg, Dan. *BASEBALL STARS 1986*. Chicago: Contemporary Books, 1986.

Schmidt, Mike, with Walder, Barbara. *ALWAYS ON THE OFFENSE*. New York: Atheneum, 1982.

Schoor, Gene. *THE TED WILLIAMS STORY*. New York: Julian Messner, 1954.

Tygiel, Jules. *BASEBALL'S GREAT EXPERIMENT—JACKIE ROBINSON AND HIS LEGACY*. New York: Oxford University Press, 1983.

Wayne, Bennett, Editor. *HEROES OF THE HOME RUN*. Champaign, Illinois: Garrard Publishing Company, 1973.

ACKNOWLEDGMENTS

In writing this book I have consulted numerous articles from the *New York Times*, the *Los Angeles Times*, *The Sporting News*, *Sport Magazine*, *Sports Illustrated*, *The 1989 World Almanac*, *People Magazine*, *Esquire*, *Ebony*, *Time*, *Newsweek*, and the *New York Times Magazine*.

Additional information came from the *Baseball Register*, the National Baseball Hall of Fame and Museum, and *The Baseball Encyclopedia*; also, media guides, yearbooks, and player statistics were furnished by the Boston Red Sox, Chicago Cubs, Oakland Athletics, Philadelphia Phillies, Minnesota Twins, San Diego Padres, San Francisco Giants, New York Yankees, Kansas City Royals, and the New York Mets.